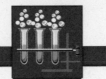

# Table of Contents

# The Scientific Method

The **scientific method** is the way scientists learn and study the world around them. You become a scientist when you try to find answers to your questions by using the scientific method.

Asking questions and coming up with answers is the basis for the scientific method. When you begin a science project, you begin with a question that you have. The educated guess you make about this question is called a **hypothesis**.

After you have asked the question and made an educated guess, you have to perform tests to determine whether or not your hypothesis is right. To test your hypothesis, you must follow a **procedure**, which is the name given to the steps you take in your experiment or fieldwork. Your experiment or fieldwork should give you information that can be measured. It is important to conduct your test multiple times and use as many test subjects as possible to make sure your results are consistent before you draw your conclusion.

Your **conclusion** describes how your **data**, or results you received from your experiment, compare to your hypothesis. A disproved hypothesis is just as important as a proven hypothesis because it gives important information to others. Your conclusion should also include any new questions that arise as you are doing your experiment.

# Chicken Little
### Physical and Earth Science

**Sleuth Question:** What do we know about the sky?

In the tale of "Chicken Little," she is hit on the head with a falling acorn. This convinces her that the sky is falling. Chicken Little then rushes off to alert the king. You might think that Chicken Little was rather silly until you know a little more about our sky. Read the sleuth notes to help learn the facts.

**Atmosphere!**

### Sleuth Notes

The sky is a part of Earth known as the **atmosphere**. It is made up of atoms of different kinds of gases. The atmosphere contains the oxygen that we breathe. It also contains the carbon dioxide that plants breathe. Our atmosphere surrounds our planet. Without the atmosphere, we would be too hot in the daytime. We would also be too cold at night. Our atmosphere insulates Earth like a blanket. It lets in and holds the right amount of the Sun's heat energy. It also protects us from the Sun's harmful rays. Our atmosphere makes life on Earth possible.

**Sleuth Fact:** The atmosphere is a blanket of gases that surrounds our planet. Our atmosphere makes life on Earth possible.

Your weight is caused by Earth's gravity. **Gravity** is the force that pulls you down to Earth. It is this pull that gives you weight. It is also the force that caused the acorn to fall and hit Chicken Little on the head. Just like you and the acorn, our atmosphere is pulled to our planet. Without gravity, the gases that make up our atmosphere would float away. The atmosphere also has weight. Because of its weight, it exerts pressure. We call this **air pressure**. If you sit on someone, your weight puts pressure on that person. The same thing happens with our atmosphere. Because the air has weight, it also puts pressure on us. On average, our atmosphere weighs 15 pounds per square inch.

**Sleuth Fact:** Earth's gravity gives the atmosphere weight. Because of its weight, the atmosphere exerts pressure.

Name: _____

# Chicken Little (cont.)

Your weight changes as you change. If you get bigger, you weigh more. If you get smaller, you weigh less. The weight of the air that makes up our atmosphere also changes. As its weight changes, the amount of pressure it puts on us changes too. Temperature can affect the weight of the air around us. Warm air weighs less than cold air. Because it weighs less, it also puts less pressure on us. Why? Warm air molecules are moving faster, causing them to take up more space. Cold air molecules move slower, taking up less space. The amount of moisture in the air can affect our atmosphere's weight. Moist air weighs less than dry air. This means that the air that makes up a hot, rainy day weighs the least. The air that makes up a very cold, dry day weighs the most. As you might expect, how high up you are also affects the air's weight and its pressure. The higher up you go, the less air there is above you. So the atmosphere's weight and pressure go down as you go higher.

 **Sleuth Fact:** The weight and pressure exerted by our atmosphere change as the air changes.

 **Pre-Lab Questions**

1. What is the atmosphere? _____

2. What does our atmosphere do?_____

3. What force gives the atmosphere weight and holds it to earth? _____

4. What is the average weight of our atmosphere? _____

5. Why does the atmosphere put pressure on us?_____

_____

6. What causes the atmosphere's weight and pressure to change? _____

_____

Name: _____

# Under Pressure

The icon  is used throughout the workbook on pages with experiments where adult supervision is strongly recommended.

**Your Investigation**

**Sleuth Question:** How much air pressure is pushing down on the top of my head?

**Materials:** a ruler, a calculator, and the top of your head

 **Procedure**

1. Use your ruler to draw a square inch on your paper. Label it 15 pounds.
2. Fill in the hypothesis on page 6 to predict the amount of pressure pushing down on your head.
3. Stand against a wall and press the back of your head against it.
4. Have someone measure the length of your head.
5. Write the measurement in the table under *length*. Remember to write *in.* beside your number.
6. Measure the width of your head.
7. Write the measurement in the table under *width*. Remember to write *in.* beside your number.
8. Multiply your head's length by its width to find the area.
9. Write the area of your head in the table under *area*. Remember to write *in.²* beside the number.
10. Multiply the area of your head by 15 to find the amount of air pressure that is pushing down on top of your head.
11. Write the amount of pressure in the table under *amount of air pressure*. Remember to write *lbs.* beside your number.
12. Add all of the numbers in the last column of your table.
13. Divide your answer by 4.
14. Write the number showing on your calculator beside the blank labeled *average*.
15. For comparison purposes, measure the person's head who helped measure your head.
16. Answer the conclusion questions.

**Draw your square inch in the space to the right.**

Name: _____

# Under Pressure (cont.)

 **Sleuth Question:** How much air pressure is pushing down on the top of my head?

**Hypothesis:** If I measure the air pressure pushing down on my head, and multiply the area of my head by 15, then the amount of pressure will be _____ lbs.

## My Data

| Name | Length of Head (in.) | Width of Head (in.) | Area of Head L x W (in.²) | Air Pressure Constant | Amount of Air |
|------|----------------------|---------------------|---------------------------|-----------------------|---------------|
|      |                      |                     |                           | x 15 lbs./in.²        |               |
|      |                      |                     |                           | x 15 lbs./in.²        |               |

## Conclusion Questions

1. Who is under more pressure? _____ Less pressure? _____

_____

2. If Chicken Little's head were 3 inches long and 2 inches wide, how much air

pressure was pushing down on her head? _____

Name: _____

# Newton's Rocker

This section of the workbook is called **physical science**. Physical science is the science of matter and energy and their interactions.

## Purpose
- This experiment will help explain how energy can be passed from object to object in inelastic collisions.
- You can observe conservation of momentum by observing movement of the objects in the activity.
- Make and operate a Newton's Rocker.

## Materials Needed
five 2-cm (about $\frac{3}{4}$ in.) wooden macramé beads          10 straws
cotton string          tape
scissors

## Introduction
The concepts of momentum, inelastic collisions, and the transfer of energy during impact are often studied by discussing automobile accidents and billiard balls. The apparatus built in this activity will work to demonstrate the concepts, but imprecise alignment and the unstable side-to-side movement will require you to observe motion immediately after the collision. Continued movement will appear to become more random.

## Procedure
See lab sheet on page 8 for instructions.

## Applications and Extensions
### Language Arts
- Investigate and write a report on what kind of safety equipment is installed on automobiles to soften the effects of collisions.

### Mathematics
- Calculate the ratio of the number of macramé beads that are pulled back to the number immediately launched from the other side.

### Social Studies
- Describe the society in which Newton lived and what may have motivated him to discover the laws of motion.

### Music
- Explore the pattern and period of time that the rocker rocks with one macramé bead swinging, two swinging, etc.

Name: _____

# Newton's Rocker

## Preparation

**1.** Tape three straws together, end to end, to form an equilateral triangle.

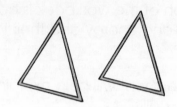

**2.** Make a second triangle by taping three more straws together.

**3.** To form the base, connect the two triangles by taping a single straw between them at the corners.

**4.** Secure a second straw by taping it to the triangles at the opposite corners from the first straw. (See illustration.) The triangles should now stand up with the single straws serving as the base.

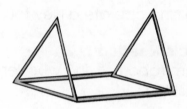

**5.** Tape two single straws together, side by side, to make a doubled straw section.

**6.** Tape the doubled straw to the third corner of each triangle to complete the cradle frame.

**7.** Cut five 30-cm (about 1 foot) pieces of cotton string.

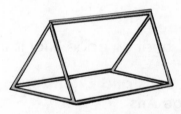

**8.** Put one end of a string through the hole in a macramé bead.

**9.** Knot the string securely to prevent it from being pulled through the hole in the bead.

**10.** Repeat Steps 8-9 for the remaining four macramé beads.

**11.** Thread the loose end of each string between and through the doubled straws from the underside of the frame. The macramé beads should hang freely.

**12.** Wrap each string around the straws to make a loop, then secure it with a knot. Continue until all five beads are hanging freely from the frame.

**13.** Adjust the macramé beads so that they are hanging at the same distance from the tabletop.

**14.** Space the beads apart so they lightly touch adjacent beads.

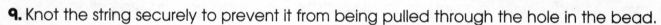

**PHYSICAL SCIENCE**

Name: _____

## Procedure

1. Pull one macramé bead back, let go, and observe how many macramé beads are immediately moved to the other side as a result of the collision.
2. Repeat with two beads.
3. Repeat with three beads.
4. Find out what happens to the energy if paper towels are folded and placed between the macramé beads. Repeat Steps 1 and 2.

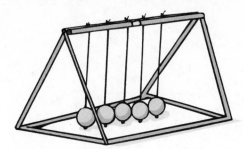

## Questions

1. How many macramé beads bounced away from the others when only one bead was pulled back?_____

2. How many macramé beads bounced away from the others when two beads were pulled back? _____

3. How many macramé beads bounced away from the others when three beads were pulled back? _____

4. Describe the energy transfer when only one bead is pulled back._____
_____

5. Describe what happens to the momentum of the bead pulled back when it hits the others. _____
_____

6. What happens to the energy when paper towels are folded and placed between the macramé beads? _____
_____

7. What makes the other macramé beads begin to move if the system is permitted to continue to move? _____
_____

8. What might make the system work better?_____
_____

Science Grade 6

Name: _____

# Insulating an Ice Cube

## Purpose
- To define the concept of insulation and explain where and why insulation is used.
- To construct a compartment that insulates an ice cube to prevent it from melting.

## Materials Needed
Styrofoam peanuts
Styrofoam containers
tape
plastic wrap
paper
various other craft materials
large ice cube
resealable plastic bag

## Introduction
Insulation does one of two things: it either prevents heat from escaping or it prevents a material from absorbing heat. In this activity, you will design and construct compartments that act as insulators and prevent ice cubes from melting. It is necessary to gather a variety of craft materials, Styrofoam trays, and containers for the constructions.

## Procedure
1. What are thermoses used for? What kinds of foods are stored in thermoses?
2. What is "insulation"? What objects act as insulators? What types of materials are used?
3. See instructions on lab sheet on page 12 for constructing the containers.
4. After the containers are tested, determine which container is the best insulator for preventing an ice cube from melting.

## Behind the Scenes
Materials such as Styrofoam serve as good insulation devices. However, air around the object will either help or hinder the outcome depending on its temperature. An example is double-paned windows that have a layer of air between them. The air between these panes of glass serves as a buffer. Try to surround the ice cube with some type of material that will act as an insulator.

Name: _____

## Applications and Extensions
### Science
- Determine which type of windows (glass, double-paned, treated) would be best at keeping a house either cool with air conditioning or warm with heat. Conduct an investigation with different windows. Tape a thermometer to each window and place the window against a lightbulb. Determine how long it takes for the temperature of the glass to increase five degrees.
- Repeat this investigation with different picnic coolers and larger blocks of ice. Place the same-sized block of ice into each picnic cooler. Set the coolers in the sunshine. Find out which block of ice melts first and which one melts last.
- Survey your home to find out how energy needs can be reduced or are being reduced by using different insulation materials or energy-efficient appliances.

### Mathematics
- Research the energy cost savings for different brands of large appliances. Find out what the savings would be if specific appliances were used for five, ten, and twenty years. Record your findings on a graph.

### Language Arts
- Develop a persuasive argument for or against the use of Styrofoam as an insulation material.

Name: _____

# Insulating an Ice Cube

Your challenge (if you should choose to accept it) is to design an insulated container that will prevent an ice cube from melting.

## Procedure

1. Brainstorm ideas on what type of container could be used, the materials needed for construction, and the design of the container.
2. On another sheet of paper, sketch your container and describe the materials to be used and its shape, size, and color. (Yes, the color of the container is important.)
3. Complete the construction of your ice cube insulator.
4. Explain the reasons for your choices.
5. Test your container.
6. Place an ice cube inside a resealable plastic bag and then set the ice cube in your container. Start the clock. Observe the ice cube several times. Record your observations on the chart.

| Time | Ice Cube Illustration | Observations |
|---|---|---|
| 2 minutes | | |
| 5 minutes | | |
| 10 minutes | | |
| 12 minutes | | |

## Questions

1. What materials did you use to build the container?_____
   _____
   Why did you choose these materials? _____
   _____
2. What other things are made with this type of material as insulation? _____
   _____
3. Describe how well your container worked in insulating the ice cube. What improvements can be made to it? _____
   _____
4. Name some item in your house that is insulated. Draw this item and explain where the insulation is used and its role. _____
   _____

Name: _____

# Generating Electricity

## Purpose
• To produce an electrical current using wire and a magnet.
• To use a magnetic compass to observe an electrical current by detecting the accompanying magnetic field it causes.

## Materials Needed
12 meters (about 40 ft.) of copper "bell" wire (bare wire)
small magnetic compass
strong bar magnet
scissors
tape
various magnets

## Introduction
An electrical current is always accompanied by a magnetic field that surrounds the wire carrying the current. In this activity, you will generate an electrical current by passing a magnet through several coils of wire. The current will be detected by deflection in the reading of a simple magnetic compass. Real power generators make electricity in a similar fashion, but it is usually the turns of wire that are passed through the magnet to generate the power rather than, as in this activity, the other way around.

## Procedure
See lab sheet on page 14 for instructions.

## Applications and Extensions
### Language Arts
• Write a story about a time when the power was interrupted and there was no electricity.

### Art
• Create a collage with pictures clipped from magazines of electrically powered items that are used in everyday life.

### Social Studies
• Research the population growth in particular regions, such as the southwestern United States, following the invention and development of the electrical power industry.

# Generating Electricity

## Procedure

1. Coil about 50 loops of wire around your hand.
2. Slip the coil off your hand and fasten it in three places with sticky tape to keep the coil tight.
3. Wrap 20 loops tightly around the compass.
4. Twist the ends of the wire together to close the circuit.
5. Separate the coil of wire and the compass (with the loops of wire around it) as far as possible so that the magnet does not directly affect the reading on the compass.

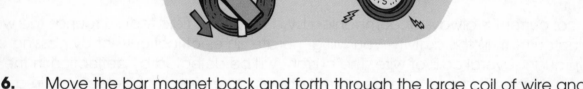

6. Move the bar magnet back and forth through the large coil of wire and notice the deflection in the needle of the compass.
7. Repeat the activity with fewer loops in the large coil of wire. Record your observations.
8. Repeat the activity with more loops in the large coil of wire. Record your observations.
9. Repeat Step 7 with different magnets to see if this has an effect. Record your observations.

## Questions

1. What deflects the needle of the compass? _____
2. What occurs if the number of loops in the coil are reduced?_____
   _____
3. Why do commercial power plants have coils with thousands of loops? _____
   _____
4. What occurs if the size of the magnet is changed? _____
   _____
5. Why do commercial power plants have magnets that weigh tons? _____
   _____

Name: _____

# Growing Crystals

## Purpose
• To recognize crystal growth as a function of chemical activity by conducting the activity.
• To explain how atoms control crystal growth by their size and arrangement.

## Materials Needed
water                                food coloring                        laundry bluing
coal or charcoal                     salt                                 balance
graduated cylinder (50 mL)           125 mL beaker
ammonia                              glass pie plate (or similar container)

## Introduction
One of nature's most beautiful creations is a repeating arrangement of atoms called a **crystal**. The crystal takes its composition and form from the particular combination of chemical elements. The atoms of each molecule, tied together with chemical bonds, arrange themselves in repeating units as the solid forms. The shape of the crystal grows as these units repeat often enough to become visible. Characteristics of the material, such as the way it reflects and conducts light through it, and even the way it breaks, are provided by the crystalline nature of the material. Although this activity will not produce diamonds (nature's most protected crystalline material), the crystal growth, the similarity of shape, and size are clearly evident.

## Procedure
See lab sheet on page 16 for instructions.

## Behind the Scenes
It is very important that the mixture is not disturbed. While crystals may begin to grow very quickly, it is possible that the mixture may take some time to begin to crystallize. By limiting the disturbances, the crystal shapes can begin to grow on an atomic level.

## Applications and Extensions
### Language Arts
• Write a paper on a gem, crystal, or mineral of your choice.
### Science
• Find out how to make large salt or sugar crystals. Then, produce your own crystals.
### Social Studies
• Report on the regions of the world that are responsible for providing your birthstone. Indicate on a map where precious and semi-precious gems are mined.
### Art
• Draw a picture that represents your birthstone, including crystal shape if it has one. Using toothpicks, create a model of the crystal shape of your choice.

Name: _____

# Growing Crystals

## Procedure

1. Using the graduated cylinder, measure 10 mL of laundry bluing. Then, pour it into the beaker.
2. Measure 50 mL of water and add it to the beaker.
3. Using the balance, measure 150 mL of salt and add it to the beaker.
4. Using the graduated cylinder, measure 20 mL of ammonia and add it to the beaker.
5. Place several small pieces of coal in the pie plate.
6. Carefully pour the mixture from the beaker over the coal.
7. Add several drops of food coloring on the pieces of coal. Perhaps different colors might be tried on different pieces of coal.
8. Place the pie plate in a area where it will not be disturbed but can be observed.
9. Observe the pie plate twice daily and record on the data sheet.

| Day | Morning | Afternoon |
|-----|---------|-----------|
| 1 | | |
| 2 | | |
| 3 | | |
| 4 | | |

## Questions

1. How long did it take for crystals to begin to grow, and where did they grow?

_____

2. What are the shapes of the crystals that grew?

_____

3. Did the food coloring have any effect on the size, shape, or color of the crystals?

_____

Name: _____

# What Color Is That Color?

## Purpose
- To apply the principle of chromatography in analyzing the black ink of water-soluble markers.
- To identify the colored inks used to make the color black for different water-soluble markers.

## Materials Needed
black water-soluble markers (by different manufacturers)
paper towels
tall, clear plastic cups
water
paper clips

## Introduction
You will discover that the color black may be made up of a number of other ink colors, and one manufacturer's black may differ significantly from another manufacturer's. This activity uses paper towels and water to separate the ink colors of water-soluble markers. This process is called **chromatography**. Inks of different densities are carried upward by the capillary action of the water as it moves through the paper towel.

## Procedure
See the lab sheet on page 18 for instructions.

## Applications and Extensions
### Language Arts
- Write a story about a court trial in which paper chromatography is used to prove the identity of the writer of a threatening note.

### Social Studies
- Research how old documents are protected against decay of the type investigated in this activity.

### Art
- Create colorful images using large ink spots in the center of a paper towel to which is added a spoonful of water.
- Using the colors available in a watercolor set, try to invent a new formula for the color black or brown.

Name: _____

# What Color Is That Color?

## Procedure

1. Cut a paper towel strip approximately one and one-half times the height of the cup being used.
2. Place a dot of ink in the center of the towel strip about $\frac{1}{2}$ in. from the end of the towel.
3. Place about $\frac{1}{2}$ in. of water in the bottom of the cup.
4. Carefully place the end of the paper towel strip with the ink spot into the cup so that only the edge of the strip touches the water.
5. Do not immerse the ink spot, but allow the water to soak up the towel across the spot.
6. Bend the other end of the paper towel strip over the lip of the cup. Use the paper clip to secure it in place.
7. Observe the strip as the rising water spreads out the various colors of the ink.
8. Draw a diagram and label the colors that are separated from the black ink.
9. Repeat the activity with two other markers made by other companies.

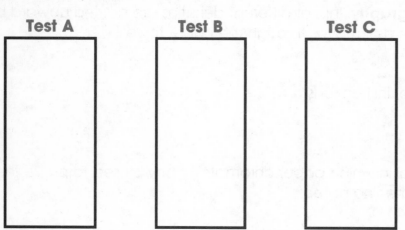

Test A          Test B          Test C

## Questions

1. Which black marker seems to be the darkest black color to you? _____

2. What black color seems to you to be the lightest? _____

3. What colors of ink are in the darkest black color? _____

4. What colors are in the lightest black color? _____

5. How could you use these strips as keys for identification? _____

_____

Name: _____

# Flowers

This section of the workbook is called **life science**. Life science is any of the branches of natural science dealing with the structure and behavior of living organisms.

Flowers have the important function of producing seeds. The male part of a flower is called the **stamen**. At the tip of the stamen is the **anther**, a tiny case with many grains of **pollen**. The female part of a flower is called the **pistil**. The tip of the pistil is the **stigma**, the long neck is the **style**, and the large base is the **ovary**. The ovary holds the tiny **ovules**, which develop into seeds.

Label the parts of the flower using the words in bold from above.

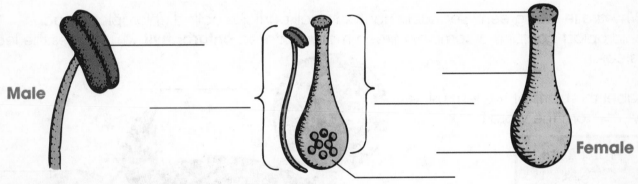

Male

Female

Complete each sentence with the missing word.
1. The anther is filled with ___ ___ ___ ___ ___ ___.
                                                                    1
2. The stigma is held up by the ___ ___ ___ ___ ___.

3. The female flower part is the ___ ___ ___ ___ ___ ___.
                                                          2              6
4. Seeds form in the ___ ___ ___ ___ ___.
                                          5
5. Seeds develop from tiny ___ ___ ___ ___ ___ ___.
                                                      3
6. The tip of the pistil is the ___ ___ ___ ___ ___ ___.
                                              8       4
7. The male flower part is the ___ ___ ___ ___ ___ ___.
                                                    7

## Something Special
Use the numbered letters to answer the riddle.

"If April showers bring May flowers, what do May flowers bring?

___ ___ ___ ___ ___ ___ ___ ___
 1    2    3    4    5    6    7    8

Science Grade 6

Name: _____

# Food Factories

Leaves are like little factories designed to do an important job—make food. Different parts of the leaf help with this job. The **veins** in a leaf are bundles of tiny tubes. They carry water and minerals to the leaf and take food from the leaf to the rest of the plant. Veins also help hold the leaf up.

On the underside of the leaf are small openings called **stomata**. Stomata have been called the lungs of a leaf because they allow **air** to enter the leaf.

The outer layers of the leaf are covered with a **waxy** layer which prevents the leaf from drying out.

Why are leaves green? Leaf cells contain small particles called chloroplasts. Each chloroplast contains a complex, green material called **chlorophyll** which gives the leaf its color.

Label the parts of the leaf using words from the word bank.

**Word Bank**
veins
stomata
waxy layer

Complete the puzzle using the words in bold.

**Across**
2. Bundles of tiny tubes that carry water, minerals, and food
4. Openings in a leaf allow _____ to enter.
5. Substance that gives a leaf its green color

**Down**
1. Surface of a leaf feels _____.
3. Small openings on the underside of the leaf

Name: _____

# Tree History

A freshly cut tree stump can be read like a tree's own personal diary. By looking closely at the rings, called **annual rings**, you can interpret clues that tell you about the tree's life.

Each ring in a tree represents one year of growth. Wide light rings usually indicate that the tree had a good growing season. Rings that are close together indicate years of slow growth. Scars and cuts may mean that the tree was in a fire or struck by lightning.

The tree pictured on this page was cut just last week. How much can you learn about its life?

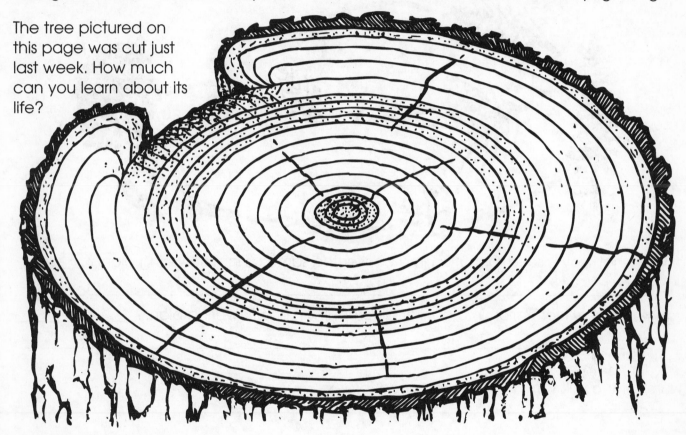

**1.** How old is this tree?_____

**2.** What year was it planted? _____

**3.** With a blue pencil or crayon, color the ring of the year you were born.

**4.** Color the rings of the slow growing years *red*.

**5.** What could have caused this slow growth? _____

_____

**6.** What could have caused the large scar on the tree? _____

_____

Name: _____

# Cone-Bearing Plants

Plants, like pine trees, that develop seeds in cones are called **conifers**. Conifers have two kinds of cones. The smaller male cone develops pollen grains. Egg cells develop in the ovule of the much larger female cone. Pollen from the male cone is carried by the wind and lodges in the scales of the female cone. A pollen tube grows down to the ovule, and a new seed is formed. After the seeds are ripe, the cone and the seed drop to the ground.

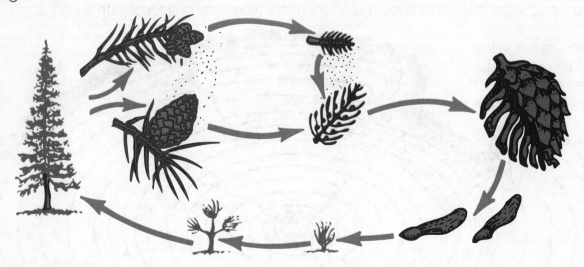

**1.** In what way is seed formation in a conifer the same as in a flowering plant? _____
_____

**2.** How is seed formation in a conifer different than in a flowering plant?_____
_____

Number the following steps in the correct order.

_____ A seed is formed.

_____ A new conifer sprouts from the seed.

_____ Pollen grains are carried by the wind.

_____ A pollen tube grows down to the ovule.

_____ Pollen grains lodge in the scales of the female cone.

_____ Ripened seeds are released from the cone.

## Fun Facts

The giant redwood trees are unquestionably the world's tallest trees. The largest of these conifers, found in Humboldt County, California, has been measured at over 300 feet tall.

Name: _____

# Backbone or No Backbone?

The animal kingdom can be divided into two groups, **vertebrates** and **invertebrates**. Vertebrates are animals with backbones. The backbone is made of several bones called **vertebrae**. Each vertabra is separated by a thin disc of cartilage. The backbone supports the body and helps the animal move.

Invertebrates are animals without backbones. Have you ever looked closely at an ant or fly? They do not have a backbone or any other bones in their bodies. Some invertebrates, like crabs and lobsters, have hard, outer-body coverings. Some invertebrates, like worms, are soft all the way through their bodies.

Circle all of the hidden animals in the puzzle below. Then, list them in their own group.

**Word Bank**

| | |
|---|---|
| butterfly | skunk |
| cow | snail |
| crayfish | snake |
| deer | spider |
| dog | swan |
| fish | wasp |
| grasshopper | worm |

```
N J W O R M E Z R A C D
G R A S S H O P P E R E
F K B P D S W A N P A E
S N A I L Q W C S X Y R
K E V D O G A I N C F G
U P S E A J S S A O I X
N O L R W M P H K F S C
K T F I S H G B E Y H O
U B U T T E R F L Y T W
```

**Vertebrates**                    **Invertebrates**

_____    _____

_____    _____

_____    _____

_____    _____

_____    _____

_____    _____

**Find Out**
About 1,000,000 kinds of animals have been classified by scientists. Only 45,000 are vertebrates. How many are invertebrates? _____

Name: _____

# Warm and Cold-Blooded Animals

Mammals and birds are **warm-blooded** animals. Warm-blooded animals maintain a constant body temperature with the help of hair or feathers as insulation. Warm-blooded animals are called **endothermic** animals.

**Cold-blooded** animals, such as fish, reptiles, and amphibians, get their body heat from their surroundings. Their body temperature varies according to the temperature of their environment. Cold-blooded animals are called **ectothermic** animals.

Circle all of the animals in the word search below using the words from the word bank. Then, list the animals in the proper group.

| **Word Bank** | |
|---|---|
| bear | rat |
| deer | salamander |
| duck | shark |
| eagle | snake |
| fox | toad |
| frog | trout |
| lizard | turtle |
| owl | |

```
I E K M O W L D B U
S A L A M A N D E R
T G I A S L T O A D
U L Z F H D E E R S
R E A R A U O E G N
T R R O R C F O X A
L A D G K K P F N K
E T R O U T B R M E
```

## Warm-Blooded

| **Mammal** | **Bird** |
|---|---|
| | |
| | |
| | |
| | |

## Cold-Blooded

| **Fish** | **Reptile** | **Amphibian** |
|---|---|---|
| | | |
| | | |
| | | |
| | | |

**Find Out**

Mammals cool off by sweating. Horses sweat through their skin, and coyotes sweat through their tongues when panting. How do your family pets cool off? How do they stay warm?

Name: _____

# Survival

An adult frog lays hundreds of eggs at one time. You would think that most ponds would be overrun with frogs. Many of these eggs will hatch, but very few offspring will survive. Most will be eaten by larger animals. Only the fittest survive. The fittest are those that **adapt** to their environment.

What does **adapt** mean? _____

_____

_____

What adaptations help each of these animals survive?

deer _____

mouse _____

skunk _____

rabbit _____

turtle _____

porcupine _____

## Something Special

Create an animal of your own. Give your animal some special defense adaptations.

animal's name _____     enemies _____

habitat _____     defenses _____

food _____     _____

Name: _____

# Food Chains

In the woodland and aquatic communities, there are a large number of food chains. Study the picture on this page.

Find at least three food chains in the scene above. List the food chains below.

| Food Chain #1 | Food Chain #2 | Food Chain #3 |
| --- | --- | --- |
| _____ | _____ | _____ |
| _____ | _____ | _____ |
| _____ | _____ | _____ |
| _____ | _____ | _____ |
| _____ | _____ | _____ |

**Find Out**

The use of DDT, a chemical insecticide, has been made illegal in many areas. What effect did this poison have on the eagle? How did this affect the eagle population?

Name: _____

# Animal Facts

Finish the puzzle below using the words from the word bank.

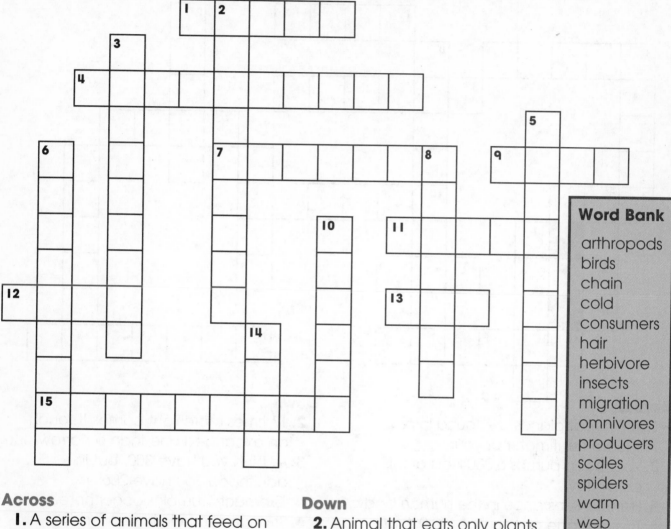

**Word Bank**

arthropods
birds
chain
cold
consumers
hair
herbivore
insects
migration
omnivores
producers
scales
spiders
warm
web

**Across**

1. A series of animals that feed on each other is a food _____.
4. Invertebrates with jointed legs
7. Largest group of invertebrates
9. Reptiles are _____-blooded.
11. Feathered, warm-blooded vertebrates
12. Body covering of mammals
13. Interlocking food chains form a food _____.
15. Organisms that eat both plants and animals

**Down**

2. Animal that eats only plants
3. Organisms that make their own food
5. Organisms that do not make their own food
6. Seasonal movement of animals
8. Arthropods with eight legs, two body sections, and no antennae
10. Body covering of reptiles
14. Birds and mammals are _____-blooded animals.

Name: _____

# Body Trivia

Test your knowledge of the human body with these amazing facts.

## Across

1. 105 sweat glands are found in one square centimeter of your _____.
3. Your heart pumps 6,000 liters of this each day.
5. Hardest substance in the human body
6. The average person has 100,000 of these on his or her head.
8. You do this with your eyes.
10. Your mouth makes $\frac{1}{2}$ liter of this each day.
12. The smallest bones of the body are located here.
13. You breathe 12,000 liters of this each day.
14. Filters 1,500 liters of blood each day
15. It takes more of these to frown than smile.

## Down

2. 17 times more light comes through an expanded one than a narrow one.
3. At birth you have 300, but in adulthood you have 206.
4. "Stomach" rumbles occur here.
6. Strongest muscle in your body
7. Only part of the body with taste buds
9. They give you stereo vision.
11. Receives 100 million nerve messages from your senses each second

Name: _____

# How Clouds Are Formed

This section of the workbook is called **earth science**. Earth science is any of the sciences dealing with earth and its parts, including outer space.

## Purpose
• To list the components necessary for cloud formation.
• To use the needed components to model cloud formation.
• To apply knowledge of the components for cloud formation to answer questions regarding clouds in our environment.

## Materials Needed
clear plastic bottle with cap
incense to use as smoke source
water

## Procedure
See lab sheet on page 30 for instructions.

## Applications and Extensions
### Language Arts
• Write stories about pictures you see in the clouds by writing a descriptive essay.

### Art
• Create a drawing, picture, mural, or 3-D diorama portraying the images you see in cloud formations.
• Identify the variety of blue hues using paint sample cards from the hardware or paint store.

### Social Studies
• Research the effect of geography on the development of clouds, including such terms as *land breeze, sea breeze, windward,* and *leeward.*
• Research the effect of human activity on the development of clouds (e.g., acid rain, cloud seeding, and effects of cooling towers).

Name: _____

# How Clouds Are Formed

## Procedure

1. Place 50 mL (1.7 oz.) of water inside a plastic bottle.
2. Shake the bottle, squeeze it hard for 15 seconds, then suddenly stop squeezing it.
3. Describe the interior of the bottle.
4. Uncap the bottle. While squeezing the bottle, place the mouth of the bottle near the burning incense. Stop squeezing so that some of the smoke enters the bottle. Recap the bottle.
5. Shake the bottle, squeeze it for 15 seconds, and then stop squeezing.
6. Describe the interior of the bottle with low pressure.
7. Now, squeeze the bottle tightly and hold for 15 seconds.
8. Describe the interior of the bottle under pressure.

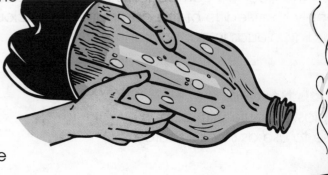

## Questions

1. Do water and pressure changes alone cause clouds to form? _____

   _____

2. What is necessary, in addition to water and pressure changes, to form a cloud?

   _____

3. Pressure changes can be caused by changes in altitude. What function does a mountain range serve in the formation of clouds? _____

   _____

4. Why do some farmers believe that putting smoke into the air can cause the formation of clouds? _____

   _____

Name: _____

# Tornado in a Bottle

## Purpose
• To observe the formation of a "tornado" due to the movement of water and air.
• To discuss why this model is representative of what occurs during a real tornado.

## Materials Needed
two 2-liter soda bottles
PVC pipe (opening fits over mouth of soda bottle)
water
rubber sealant

## Procedure
See lab sheet on page 32 for instructions.

## Behind the Scenes
If you live in the northern hemisphere, rotate the bottle counterclockwise to show how tornadoes spin. The rotation of the earth on its axis causes tornadoes to spin counterclockwise in that hemisphere. If you were to encounter a tornado in the southern hemisphere, it would spin clockwise.

As water from the top bottle begins to fall into the bottom bottle, it displaces the air and pushes it upward. When the bottle is shaken in a counterclockwise motion, the water molecules fall in a circular motion, leaving the center column for air to quickly move into the upper bottle. Although scientists are not sure of the conditions under which a tornado occurs, it is more likely when a cold, dry air mass moves underneath a warm, moist air mass. In this case, the water represents the warm, moist air mass and the air represents the cold, dry air mass. As the lighter air mass (air in the bottle) rapidly moves up through the heavier air mass (water), a low pressure system forms in the center (column of air).

## Applications and Extensions
### Geography
• Research where "Tornado Alley" is and why this section of the United States has been given this name.

### Math
• After identifying Tornado Alley, determine the average number of tornados per year. Develop a key and color code the states appropriately to show a picture graph.

### Health and Safety
• Locate literature on tornado safety and discuss ways to be safe during a severe storm.

Science Grade 6

Name: _____

# Tornado in a Bottle

## Setup

1. To make the tornado bottle, fill one of the soda bottles to the very top of the neck with water.
2. Line the inside of the PVC piping with rubber sealant and place it over the mouth of the first bottle.
3. Line the outside of the mouth of the second bottle with rubber sealant and insert the bottle mouth into the PVC piping.
4. Carefully hold the bottles upright and place in a location to dry overnight.

## Preparation

1. Holding the top bottle, begin to rotate it in a counterclockwise shaking motion. The water will begin to turn, forming a funnel-shaped column of air in the center.
2. Record your observations as to the shape of the funnel, whether or not it remains the same during the activity, and whether it stays oriented in the same direction.

## Questions

1. In which direction does the water rotate as it drains from one bottle to the other?

   _____

   _____

2. Does a "tornado" always move in the same ways from one demonstration to the next? _____

   _____

Name: _____

# What Causes Day and Night?

## Purpose
• To explain how the rotation of the Earth causes day and night by observing shadows.
• To describe the direction the Earth rotates on its axis.

## Materials Needed
| | |
|---|---|
| a long stick | clear, sunny area |
| plastic discs or other markers | hammer |
| grease pencil | compass |
| colored pencils | paper |

## Introduction
The rotation of the Earth on its axis results in the Sun's rays striking the Earth at different points and times. Because of this rotation, part of the Earth at any given time is not receiving sunlight and part of it is, thus causing day and night to occur.

## Procedure
See lab sheet on page 34 for instructions.

## Behind the Scenes
The Earth rotates in a counterclockwise motion, or from west to east, which causes objects in the sky to appear that they are moving from east to west. This explains why it appears that the Sun rises in the east, moves across the sky, and sets in the west.

## Applications and Extensions
### Math
• Create a graph that represents the times of sunrise and sunset each day. Compare your results over a period of time.
• Using information on time zones, determine the time in other parts of the world.

### Language Arts
• Write where you think the Sun goes at night and the adventures it has.

### Art
• Trace your shadow on the playground with chalk at different times of the day. Discuss why your shadow gets "longer" and "shorter" depending on where the Sun is in the sky.

### Social Studies
• List ten major cities in the world. Determine the time zone for each city.

Name: _____

# What Causes Day and Night?

## Setup

1. Hammer the stick into the ground so that it will stand upright and perpendicular to the ground.
2. Using your compass, determine north. Place a marker with an *N* on it on the north side of the stick.
3. Mark the other three cardinal points with plastic discs that have been labeled *S*, *E*, and *W*.
4. The stick will cast a shadow on the ground somewhere. Mark the end point of the shadow with a plastic disc or other marker. Write the time on the marker with a grease pencil.

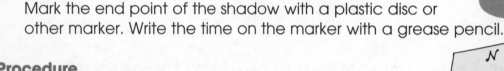

## Procedure

1. On a sheet of paper, make a chart that shows the compass directions. See the diagram.
2. Using a black crayon or colored pencil, draw on your chart where the stick's shadow is cast on the ground. Label the time.
3. Where will the shadow be cast after ten minutes? Using a red pencil or crayon, draw your prediction and label it on your chart.
4. After ten minutes, observe where the shadow is located. Place a marker at the tip of the stick's shadow. Using the grease pencil, write the time on the marker. On your chart, use a blue pencil or crayon to draw the position of the shadow and label its time.
5. Continue to observe the shadow at various times. After markers have been placed on the ground throughout the day, record your observations on the chart.

## Questions

1. Toward which direction did you predict the stick's shadow would move?_____ Which direction did it move? _____ Based on this prediction and observation, describe the direction the shadow will move for the rest of the day. Explain your answer. _____

   _____

2. Describe what you notice about the length of the stick's shadow and the time the shadow was cast._____
   When is the shadow the shortest? _____ the longest? _____ Why does the shadow's length change? _____

   _____

3. Based on your observations, describe what direction the Earth rotates and your reason. _____

   _____

Name: _____

# Why Do Stars Twinkle?

## Purpose
• To list some factors that create the twinkling effect of stars.

## Materials Needed
candle
"dirty" chalkboard eraser
flashlight
red filter or red cellophane
blue filter or blue cellophane

## Introduction
Observatories are often located in remote and high areas so that the effects of air pollution, heat pollution of the air, and light pollution do not distract from the observation. This lab activity attempts to demonstrate the negative effects of each of these types of pollution on the quality of different kinds of light that can be observed coming from a flashlight. You will discover that not all wavelengths of light are affected by pollution to the same degree.

## Procedure
See lab sheet on page 36 for instructions.

## Applications and Extensions
### Social Studies
• Locate and mark important observatories on a map and explain how their locations deal with the findings in the lab.

### Language Arts
• After reading the book *Twinkle, Twinkle Little Star* (Trapani), write a modern version of the nursery rhyme or other poems related to the night sky.

### Art
• Use light to create pieces of art using Lite Brite® or making suncatchers by gluing pieces of cellophane on frames to hang in your bedroom window.

Name: _____

# Why Do Stars Twinkle?

Have someone point a flashlight while you observe the following changes.

## Procedure

**1.** While the room lights are turned on, look at the flashlight's beam from across the room. Describe how it looks.

**2.** Turn out the room lights and observe the light. Does it look different? Describe it.

**3.** Clap an eraser near the flashlight. How does the dust change the way the light looks?

**4.** Put a red filter or a piece of red cellophane on the flashlight. Does the red light look brighter or duller than the light without cellophane?

Is the red light brighter as it passes through chalk dust? _____

**5.** Put a blue filter or a piece of blue cellophane on the flashlight. Does the blue light look brighter or duller than the light without cellophane?

Is the blue light brighter as it passes through chalk dust? _____

 **6.** Observe what happens when an adult lights a candle and places it about 4 in. In front of the flashlight. How bright is the beam of light as it passes through the heat coming from the candle?

## Questions

**1.** Why are astronomical observatories often found on hilltops? _____

_____

**2.** Why are astronomical observatories often found in remote areas? _____

_____

## page 4
1. The atmosphere is a protective blanket of air that surrounds our planet.
2. It insulates Earth, protects us from the Sun's harmful rays, provides oxygen for us to breathe, and makes life on Earth possible.
3. gravity
4. 15 pounds per square inch
5. because gravity is pulling it down giving it weight
6. temperature and amount of moisture in the air

## page 6
1. Answers will vary depending on data.
2. 90 pounds of air pressure

## page 9
1. One
2. Two
3. Three
4. The energy needed to move a single bead is transferred from bead to bead until one bead bounces away from the other.
5. The momentum is passed to the end bead that bounces away from the others.
6. The paper towels absorb the energy (by deforming), causing the beads to not bounce as well as in the previous trial.
7. The energy exchange is not perfect, and the frame may also begin to move.
8. A heavier frame and heavier beads might make the system work better.

## page 12
1. Answers will vary.
2. Answers will vary.

3. Answers will vary.
4. Answers will vary. For example, a refrigerator or thermos bottle is insulated.

## page 14
1. A magnetic field set up by an electrical current
2. The deflection on the compass was reduced when a weaker current was generated.
3. They need to produce vast quantities of current.
4. If the magnet is changed to a larger size, the current increases.
15. The size of the magnet influences the current produced and power plants need to produce large amounts of current.

## page 16
1. Answers will vary. For example, crystals will begin to form within a day or two depending on the conditions of air temperature and humidity.
2. Answers will vary according to observations made.
3. No. The food colorings are simply coloring agents.

## page 18
1. Answers will vary.
2. Answers will vary.
3. Answers will vary but may include the colors red, blue, brown, green, and others.
4. Answers will vary but may include the colors red, blue, brown, green, and others.
5. Because the strips vary in darkness you can tell them apart.

## page 19

### Flowers

This section of the workbook is called **life science**. Life science is any of the branches of natural science dealing with the structure and behavior of living organisms.

Flowers have the important function of producing seeds. The male part of a flower is called the **stamen**. At the tip of the stamen is the **anther**, a tiny case with many grains of **pollen**. The female part of a flower is called the **pistil**. The tip of the pistil is the **stigma**, the long neck is the **style**, and the large base is the **ovary**. The ovary holds the tiny **ovules**, which develop into seeds.

Label the parts of the flower using the words in bold from above.

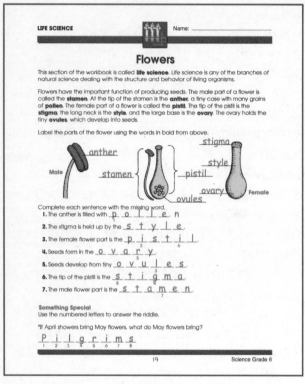

Male — anther, stamen
stigma, style, pistil, ovary, ovules
Female

Complete each sentence with the missing word.
1. The anther is filled with _p o l l e n_
2. The stigma is held up by the _s t y l e_
3. The female flower part is the _p i s t i l_
4. Seeds form in the _o v a r y_
5. Seeds develop from tiny _o v u l e s_
6. The tip of the pistil is the _s t i g m a_
7. The male flower part is the _s t a m e n_

**Something Special**
Use the numbered letters to answer the riddle.

"If April showers bring May flowers, what do May flowers bring?"

_P i l g r i m s_
1  2  3  4  5  6  7  8

19     Science Grade 6

## page 20

### Food Factories

Leaves are like little factories designed to do an important job—make food. Different parts of the leaf help with this job. The **veins** in a leaf are bundles of tiny tubes. They carry water and minerals to the leaf and take food from the leaf to the rest of the plant. Veins also help hold the leaf up.

On the underside of the leaf are small openings called **stomata**. Stomata have been called the lungs of a leaf because they allow **air** to enter the leaf.

The outer layers of the leaf are covered with a **waxy** layer which prevents the leaf from drying out.

Why are leaves green? Leaf cells contain small particles called chloroplasts. Each chloroplast contains a complex, green material called **chlorophyll** which gives the leaf its color.

Label the parts of the leaf using words from the word bank.

**Word Bank**
veins
stomata
waxy layer

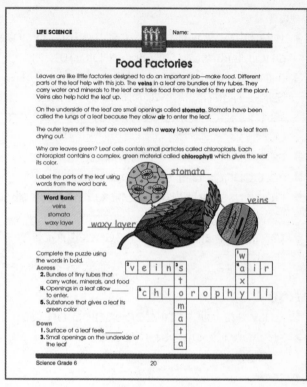

stomata
veins
waxy layer

Complete the puzzle using the words in bold.

**Across**
2. Bundles of tiny tubes that carry water, minerals, and food
4. Openings in a leaf allow _____ to enter.
5. Substance that gives a leaf its green color

**Down**
1. Surface of a leaf feels _____.
3. Small openings on the underside of the leaf

Crossword answers:
Across 2: veins
Down 1: waxy / 3: stomata
Across 4: air
Across 5: chlorophyll

Science Grade 6     20

## page 21

### Tree History

A freshly cut tree stump can be read like a tree's own personal diary. By looking closely at the rings, called **annual rings**, you can interpret clues that tell you about the tree's life.

Each ring in a tree represents one year of growth. Wide light rings usually indicate that the tree had a good growing season. Rings that are close together indicate years of slow growth. Scars and cuts may mean that the tree was in a fire or struck by lightning.

The tree pictured on this page was cut just last week. How much can you learn about its life?

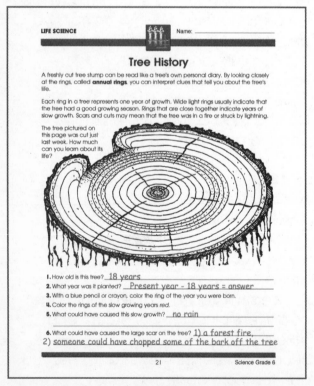

1. How old is this tree? _18 years_
2. What year was it planted? _Present year - 18 years = answer_
3. With a blue pencil or crayon, color the ring of the year you were born.
4. Color the rings of the slow growing years red.
5. What could have caused this slow growth? _no rain_

6. What could have caused the large scar on the tree? _1) a forest fire,_
_2) someone could have chopped some of the bark off the tree_

21     Science Grade 6

## page 22

### Cone-Bearing Plants

Plants, like pine trees, that develop seeds in cones are called **conifers**. Conifers have two kinds of cones. The smaller male cone develops pollen grains. Egg cells develop in the ovule of the much larger female cone. Pollen from the male cone is carried by the wind and lodges in the scales of the female cone. A pollen tube grows down to the ovule, and a new seed is formed. After the seeds are ripe, the cone and the seed drop to the ground.

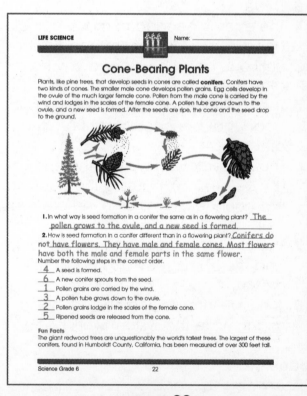

1. In what way is seed formation in a conifer the same as in a flowering plant? _The pollen grows to the ovule, and a new seed is formed._
2. How is seed formation in a conifer different than in a flowering plant? _Conifers do not have flowers. They have male and female cones. Most flowers have both the male and female parts in the same flower._

Number the following steps in the correct order.
_4_ A seed is formed.
_6_ A new conifer sprouts from the seed.
_1_ Pollen grains are carried by the wind.
_3_ A pollen tube grows down to the ovule.
_2_ Pollen grains lodge in the scales of the female cone.
_5_ Ripened seeds are released from the cone.

**Fun Facts**
The giant redwood trees are unquestionably the world's tallest trees. The largest of these conifers, found in Humboldt County, California, has been measured at over 300 feet tall.

Science Grade 6     22

# ANSWER KEY

## page 23

LIFE SCIENCE                    Name: _____

### Backbone or No Backbone?

The animal kingdom can be divided into two groups, **vertebrates** and **invertebrates**. Vertebrates are animals with backbones. The backbone is made of several bones called **vertebrae**. Each vertebra is separated by a thin disc of cartilage. The backbone supports the body and helps the animal move.

Invertebrates are animals without backbones. Have you ever looked closely at an ant or fly? They do not have a backbone or any other bones in their bodies. Some invertebrates, like crabs and lobsters, have hard, outer-body coverings. Some invertebrates, like worms, are soft all the way through their bodies.

Circle all of the hidden animals in the puzzle below. Then list them in their own group.

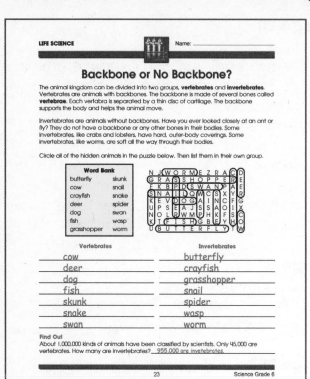

**Word Bank**

| | |
|---|---|
| butterfly | skunk |
| cow | snail |
| crayfish | snake |
| deer | spider |
| dog | swan |
| fish | wasp |
| grasshopper | worm |

| Vertebrates | Invertebrates |
|---|---|
| cow | butterfly |
| deer | crayfish |
| dog | grasshopper |
| fish | snail |
| skunk | spider |
| snake | wasp |
| swan | worm |

**Find Out**
About 1,000,000 kinds of animals have been classified by scientists. Only 45,000 are vertebrates. How many are invertebrates? _955,000 are invetebrates._

23                    Science Grade 6

## page 24

LIFE SCIENCE                    Name: _____

### Warm and Cold-Blooded Animals

Mammals and birds are **warm-blooded** animals. Warm-blooded animals maintain a constant body temperature with the help of hair or feathers as insulation. Warm-blooded animals are called **endothermic** animals.

**Cold-blooded** animals, such as fish, reptiles, and amphibians, get their body heat from their surroundings. Their body temperature varies according to the temperature of their environment. Cold-blooded animals are called **ectothermic** animals.

Circle all of the animals in the word search below using the words from the word bank. Then, list the animals in the proper group.

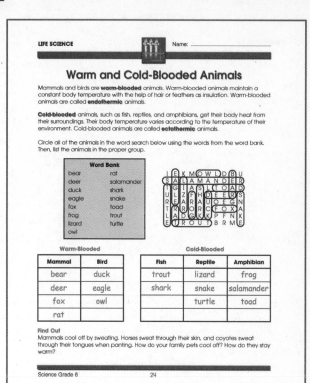

**Word Bank**

| | |
|---|---|
| bear | rat |
| deer | salamander |
| duck | shark |
| eagle | snake |
| fox | toad |
| frog | trout |
| lizard | turtle |
| owl | |

**Warm-Blooded**

| Mammal | Bird |
|---|---|
| bear | duck |
| deer | eagle |
| fox | owl |
| rat | |

**Cold-Blooded**

| Fish | Reptile | Amphibian |
|---|---|---|
| trout | lizard | frog |
| shark | snake | salamander |
| | turtle | toad |

**Find Out**
Mammals cool off by sweating. Horses sweat through their skin, and coyotes sweat through their tongues when panting. How do your family pets cool off? How do they stay warm?

Science Grade 6                    24

## page 25

LIFE SCIENCE                    Name: _____

### Survival

An adult frog lays hundreds of eggs at one time. You would think that most ponds would be overrun with frogs. Many of these eggs will hatch, but very few offspring will survive. Most will be eaten by larger animals. Only the fittest survive. The fittest are those that **adapt** to their environment.

What does **adapt** mean? _adjust to a situation to become more fit for survival_

What adaptations help each of these animals survive?
deer _quickness, excellent hearing and sense of smell, fawns bear camouflage_
mouse _quickness, small size, can see well in the dark_
skunk _excellent means of protecting self with scent glands_
rabbit _speed and good sense of hearing_
turtle _shell is excellent protection_
porcupine _sharp quills_

**Something Special**
Create an animal of your own. Give your animal some special defense adaptations.
animal's name _____ enemies _____
habitat _Answers will vary._ defenses _____
food _____

25                    Science Grade 6

## page 26

LIFE SCIENCE                    Name: _____

### Food Chains

In the woodland and aquatic communities, there are a large number of food chains. Study the picture on this page.

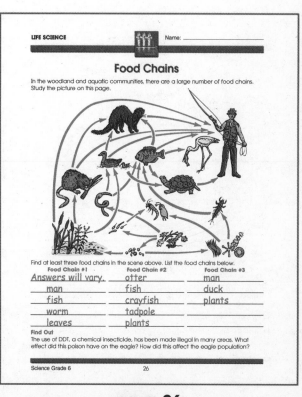

Find at least three food chains in the scene above. List the food chains below.

| Food Chain #1 | Food Chain #2 | Food Chain #3 |
|---|---|---|
| Answers will vary. | otter | man |
| man | fish | duck |
| fish | crayfish | plants |
| worm | tadpole | |
| leaves | plants | |

**Find Out**
The use of DDT, a chemical insecticide, has been made illegal in many areas. What effect did this poison have on the eagle? How did this affect the eagle population?

Science Grade 6                    26

## page 30
1. No
2. Answers will vary. For example, smoke or condensation nuclei is also necessary.
3. Answers will vary. For example, on the windward side of the mountains, air is made to rise.
4. Answers will vary. For example, if sufficient humidity is present, the smoke would serve as condensation nuclei.

## page 32
1. Counterclockwise
2. Answers may vary. For example, student may answer "yes."

## page 34
1. Answers will vary. For example, the shadow will move to the east.
2. Answers will vary. For example, the shortest shadow is visible at mid-day and lengthens during earlier and later times. The shadow's length changes as the Sun appears to move across the sky.
3. Answers will vary. For example, rotation is toward the east.

## page 36
1. Answers will vary. For example, the entire sky can be viewed.
2. Answers will vary. For example, the remote area is darker than an urban area because there is less light pollution.

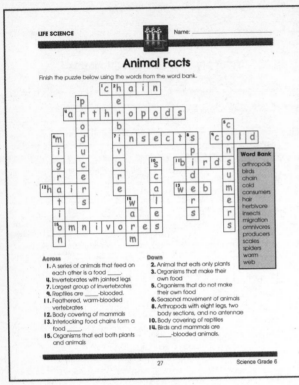

**page 27**

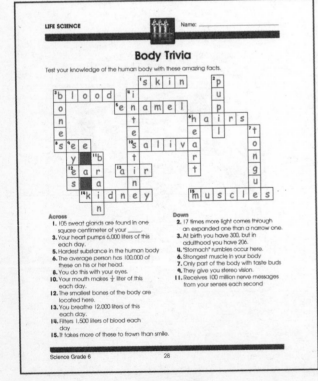

**page 28**